The Life of

Mary Seacole

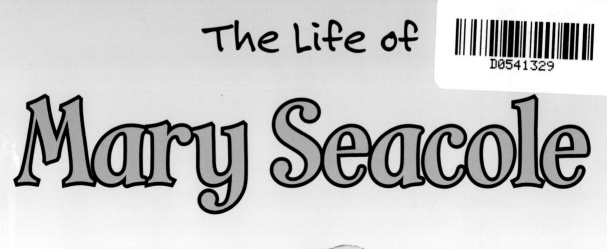

Emma Lynch

Heinemann
LIBRARY

D0541329

www.heinemann.co.uk/library

Visit our website to find out more information about **Heinemann Library** books.

To order:

☎ Phone 44 (0) 1865 888066

📄 Send a fax to 44 (0) 1865 314091

💻 Visit the Heinemann Bookshop at www.heinemann.co.uk/library to browse our catalogue and order online.

First published in Great Britain by Heinemann Library, Halley Court, Jordan Hill, Oxford OX2 8EJ, part of Harcourt Education.
Heinemann is a registered trademark of Harcourt Education Ltd.

Editorial: Lucy Thunder and Harriet Milles
Design: Richard Parker and
    Tinstar Design Ltd (www.tinstar.co.uk)
Illustrations: Jeff Edwards and Gerry Ball
    (Eikon Illustration)
Picture Research: Melissa Allison and Fiona Orbell
Production: Camilla Smith

Originated by Repro Multi-Warna
Printed and bound in China by
    South China Printing Company
The paper used to print this book comes from sustainable resources.

ISBN 0 431 18103 9 (hardback)
09 08 07 06 05
10 9 8 7 6 5 4 3 2 1

ISBN 0 431 18168 3 (paperback)
10 09 08 07 06
10 9 8 7 6 5 4 3 2 1

British Library Cataloguing in Publication Data
Emma Lynch
Mary Seacole. – (The Life of)
610.7'3'092
A full catalogue record for this book is available from the British Library.

Acknowledgements
The Publishers would like to thank the following for permission to reproduce photographs:
pp. **4, 6, 11, 20, 15** Bridgeman Art Library/Private Collection; p. **7** Michael Graham-Stewart/Bridgeman Art Library; p. **9** Mary Evans Picture Library/Bruce Castle Museum; p. **12** Bridgeman Art Library/Victoria & Albert Museum; p **13** Stanley B. Burns, MD & The Burns Archive, NY; p. **14** Science and Society Picture Library; p. **16** Fotomas Index; p. **26** The Wellcome Trust Medical Photographic Library; p. **17** Mary Evans Picture Library; p. **19** Getty Images/Hulton Archive; p. **21** Topham/Fotomas; p. **22** Amoret Tanner Collection; p. **23** The Mary Seacole Centre for Nursing Practice; pp. **24, 25** The Florence Nightingale Museum Trust; p. **27** Christopher Woods

Cover photograph of Mary Seacole, reproduced with permission of The Florence Nightingale Museum Trust. Page icon: Hemera PhotoObjects.

Every effort has been made to contact copyright holders of any material reproduced in this book. Any omissions will be rectified in subsequent printings if notice is given to the Publishers.

Contents

Words shown in the text in bold, **like this**, are explained in the Glossary.

Who was Mary Seacole?

Mary Seacole was a nurse and a **carer**. She lived in the 1800s. She travelled around the world and helped soldiers who were hurt in the **Crimean War**.

This is one of the only pictures of Mary that was painted while she was alive.

Mary did work that was normally done by doctors at that time. She saved many lives. Mary also wrote a book. It tells us much of what we know about her.

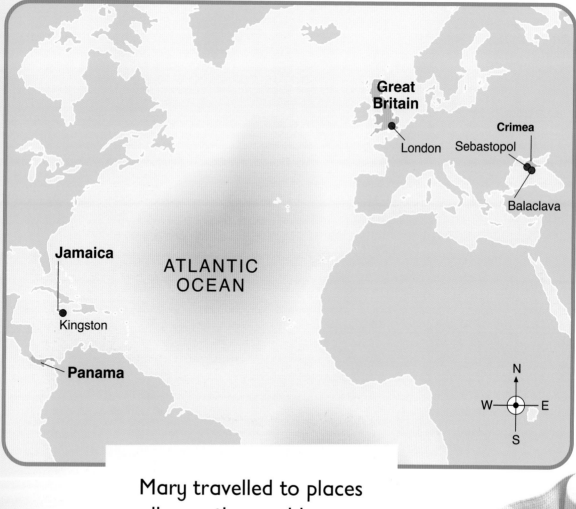

Mary travelled to places all over the world.

Growing up in Jamaica

Mary Jane Grant was born in Kingston, Jamaica in 1805. Her mother was of **mixed race**, and her father was white. He was a soldier in the British army.

This is Kingston in Jamaica in about 1835.

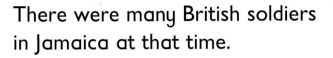

There were many British soldiers in Jamaica at that time.

Mary was brought up by her mother and her aunt. Mary's mother ran a **boarding house**. British soldiers who were ill stayed there with their families.

Early years

Mary's mother made her own medicine to help the sick soldiers get better. When she was quite young, Mary started to help her mother with her work.

Mary liked helping her mother care for soldiers who were ill.

When Mary visited
London, it looked like this.

When she was a teenager, Mary visited
London and met her father's family. Next
time Mary visited London she stayed for
two years. Then she went back to
Jamaica to help her mother.

The British Hotel

Mary married Edwin Seacole in 1836. He died soon after they got married. Then Mary's mother died. Mary opened a **boarding house**, called the British Hotel.

Mary sold jams, pickles, and food at the British Hotel.

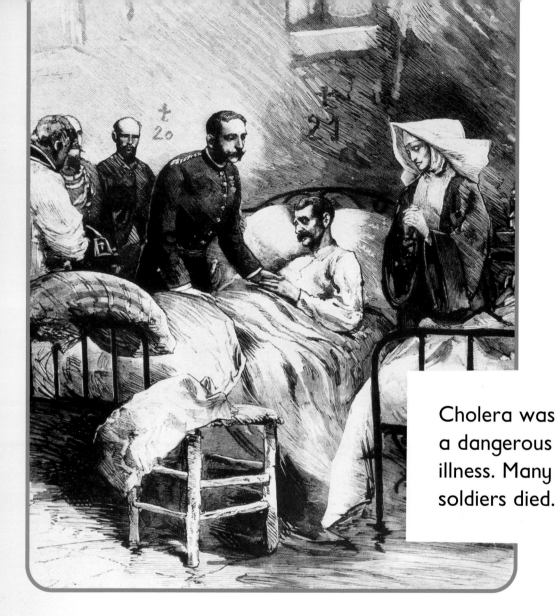

Cholera was a dangerous illness. Many soldiers died.

In 1850, Mary nursed people with an illness called **cholera** in Jamaica. Then she went to visit her brother in Panama. She nursed sick people there, too.

News of war

In 1854 Mary heard about a war in the **Crimea**. Soldiers from Britain and Jamaica were going to fight there. Mary wanted to go and help too.

These soldiers are at the British Army Camp in the Crimea.

British nurses were going to the Crimea. Mary went to Britain, but was told she was not needed. She sailed to the Crimea on her own in 1855. She was 50 years old.

Florence Nightingale was a famous British nurse who helped in the **Crimean War**.

Going to the Crimea

Mary stopped in Turkey on her way to the **Crimea**. She bought food, medicine, and other **supplies**. At last Mary arrived in the Crimea, at a place called Balaclava.

This is a picture of British and French ships at Balaclava.

Mary was soon very busy. She worked with the army doctors. She cleaned and bandaged the soldiers' **wounds**. She made cakes and handed out lemonade!

Mary would have used medicines like this to help soldiers who were in pain.

Life in the Crimea

Mary opened a store near Balaclava. It was called Spring Hill. Soldiers paid what they could for food and care. Mary used the money to buy **supplies**.

Mary's store sold clothes, boots, and shoes.

Spring Hill had a shop, a restaurant, and a small hospital. Mary nursed the soldiers from 5 a.m. until midday. Then she worked in the store until 8 p.m.

There was fierce fighting on the battlefields in Balaclava.

On the battlefield

Mary gave food and drinks to soldiers on their way into battle. Then Mary would ride on a horse to the battlefield to help nurse the **wounded** soldiers.

The soldiers called Mary 'Mother Seacole' because she looked after them so well.

Mary became friends with William H. Russell. He was a famous **war reporter** for a British newspaper.

William H. Russell called Mary 'a kind and successful **physician**' in one of his reports.

After the war

The **Crimean War** ended in 1856. The soldiers left, and Mary could not sell her **supplies**. She closed her Spring Hill stores and went back to Britain.

OUR OWN VIVANDIÈRE.

This cartoon asks people to help Mary because she did so much to help Britain.

Mary was very poor. Her friends **raised** money to help her. Mary wrote a book about her life. It was printed in 1857.

Mary's book tells us about her work in the Crimean War.

WONDERFUL ADVENTURES of Mʳˢ SEACOLE

LONDON
JAMES BLACKWOOD
PATERNOSTER ROW.

Mary's last years

Mary's last years were quiet, but she was not forgotten. People still **raised** money for her. Old soldiers would stop her in the street to thank her.

Mary spent the rest of her life in London.

This is a picture
of Mary's grave.

HERE LIES
MARY
SEACOLE
1805 – 1881

OF KINGSTON, JAMAICA
A NOTABLE NURSE WHO CARED
FOR THE SICK AND WOUNDED IN
THE WEST INDIES, PANAMA
AND ON THE BATTLEFIELDS
OF THE CRIMEA
1854 – 1856

Mary Seacole died on 14 May 1881.
She was 76 years old. She was buried
in Kensal Green in London.

Why is Mary famous?

We remember Mary because she did so much in her life. At that time, very few women travelled to dangerous places or worked with men.

Mary had no husband, and she was of **mixed race**. This would have made life hard for her.

In the early 1800s, people did not think that nursing was an important job. The work that Mary and other nurses did in the **Crimean War** changed that.

The first British **training** school for nurses opened in 1860 at St Thomas' Hospital in London.

Learn about Mary Seacole

We can learn about Mary from books and websites. We can visit **museums** and see objects from the **Crimean War**. Some nursing schools are even named after Mary.

The doctors that Mary worked with would have used tools like these.

Many people want Mary's work to be remembered. They want a statue of Mary to be built in London.

Clive Soley, **MP**, is one of the people who think a statue of Mary should be built.

Fact file

- In 1843, the Great Fire of Kingston burnt through large parts of the town. It destroyed many homes. Mary's home was burned down, and she nearly died.

- Mary received three medals for her work in the **Crimean War**.

- On 9 February 2004, Mary Seacole was voted the Greatest Black Briton of all time.

- Every year in May, the Mary Seacole Memorial Association meets at Mary's grave to remember her.

Timeline

1805   Mary Grant is born in Jamaica

1823   Mary visits London

1825   Mary goes back to Jamaica

1836   Mary marries Edwin Seacole

1850   Mary visits Panama

1854   Mary sails to the **Crimea** to care
for British soldiers fighting in the war

1856   The **Crimean War** ends.
Mary returns to live in England.

1857   Mary's book about her life is printed

1860   The first **training** school for nurses
opens in Britain

1867   Friends start to **raise** money
for Mary

1881   Mary dies in London on 14 May

Glossary

boarding house place where people pay to stay overnight, or for a longer time

carer someone who looks after people

cholera disease that people can catch from bad food or dirty water

Crimea part of the Russian Empire

Crimean War war that lasted from 1853 until 1856. Soldiers from Britain and France fought against Russian soldiers. Britain and France won the war.

MP (Member of Parliament) a person who is chosen to help run the country

mixed race someone who has one black and one white parent

museum place where important pieces of art or parts of history are kept for people to see

physician someone who makes ill people better

raise collect money or other things from many people

supplies things that people need, such as food or medicine

train teach people how to do something

war reporter someone who goes to where a war is taking place to write about it

wound very badly hurt part of the body

Find out more

Books

Famous People, Famous Lives: Mary Seacole, Harriet Castor and Lynne Willey (Franklin Watts, 2001)

Tell me about... Mary Seacole, John Malam (Evans Brothers, 1999)

Websites

www.maryseacole.com
Website of the Mary Seacole Centre.

www.bbc.co.uk/history/historic_figures/seacole_mary.shtml
BBC site about Mary Seacole's life.

Places to visit

Mary's grave at St Mary's Catholic Cemetery in London

Imperial War Museum in London

Imperial War Museum North in Manchester

Index